Introduction to Managing Change

Association for Project Management

Association for Project Management
Ibis House, Regent Park
Summerleys Road, Princes Risborough
Buckinghamshire
HP27 9LE

British Library Cataloguing in Publication Data is available.
Paperback ISBN: 978-1-903494-68-4
eISBN: 978-1-903494-69-1

Cover design by Fountainhead Creative Consultants
Typeset by RefineCatch Limited, Bungay, Suffolk
in 11/14 pt Foundry Sans

Contents

Contents

Foreword

According to a well-known textbook, a project is a combination of human and non-human resources pulled together into a temporary organisation to achieve a specified purpose. While this is fine as a formal description of what is supposed to happen in a project, it misses something about the essential part of a project – that projects are about creating a change from an existing state. The word 'project' emerged in medieval English as a design or plan from the Latin *projectum* (projecting part), which came from *proicere* 'to throw forward', which in turn came from *pro* 'from (a place)' and *iacio* 'to hurl'. The modern meaning of project emerged as it transformed from the hurling of a physical object in space to the projection of an intangible plan or design in time. Thus projects start with an idea and project management addresses the process of changing the world to match that idea. Nowadays projects are used extensively for a whole range of tasks including development of new products and services, process improvement, implementation of IT and production technologies and achieving a wide range of strategic objectives. All of these tasks involve an element of or are wholly concerned with organisational change.

Sadly, over recent years many projects have failed to deliver the promises of the original idea. There have been spectacular project failures across a range of sectors (including IT, transport, defence and construction) both in the UK and abroad. According to some leading project management academics much of this failure can be put down to senior managers and project teams underestimating, up front, the extent of uncertainty and complexity involved in their projects and failing to adapt their management style to the situation. This in turn may have resulted from the fact that much of the standard literature and professional guidance remains rooted in a mechanistic paradigm of control in which the formal tools and methods of project management help formalise attempts at optimisation. Rational methods model, plan and optimise design and development, with objective, scientific and often computerised methods seen as superior to 'soft' management techniques.

Good project managers know that formal project management tools on their own are not sufficient to ensure a successful outcome. Bad project managers and other managers who are not project managers think that if everything is done by the book then it will turn out all right. Formal tools and methods may be sufficient for simple, predictable projects. However, in a world that is becoming ever more VUCA (volatile, uncertain, complex and ambiguous) and as projects themselves become larger, more complex, more software intensive and more political, while formal tools and techniques may be necessary, they may not be sufficient. In today's environment, good project managers are men and women who have the judgement and experience to manage conflicting stakeholders' aims and objectives and act effectively in the face of a constant stream of unpredictable problems. This depends on understanding local context, the open-ended and fluid nature of problems and the practical details about what it is reasonable to expect to work. As such, the knowledge required to manage projects includes a large tacit and subjective element and is typically widely distributed around, within and outside a core project management team. Moreover, it is reflexive as it must address peoples' behaviour and also how they understand themselves and their roles.

I therefore welcome the APM's *Introduction to Managing Change*, which recognises that the tools and methods which can be used for simple, predictable projects need to be supplemented with knowledge about how to manage the change which is an inevitable part of the process of today's complex projects. Integrating this additional knowledge with their existing P3 disciplines should help today's project professionals deliver successful outcomes and projects that realise their intended benefits.

Professor Tim Brady
Centre for Research in Innovation Management
Brighton Business School, University of Brighton

Acknowledgements

This publication has been prepared by the APM Enabling Change Specific Interest Group (SIG) under its chair Martin Taylor. The authors are 2016–17 committee members Tim Beaumont, Parag Gogate, Elisabeth Goodman, David Packham, Martin Taylor and Simon Williams.

The APM Enabling Change SIG is grateful for the contributions and feedback received from across APM, in particular the Benefits, People and Programme Management SIGs and the North West and South Wales and West of England branches. *Managing Change* is ultimately all about its practical application and as such the authors are extremely appreciative of all the organisations and individuals which have participated in research or provided ideas, experience or feedback through the SIG's industry sector change practitioner groups and other forums.

1

Purpose

This *Introduction to Managing Change* first edition has been produced by the Enabling Change Specific Interest Group (SIG) of the Association for Project Management (APM). The purpose of this publication is to introduce the importance of managing change[1] effectively in order to successfully deliver and realise the benefits of projects, programmes and portfolios (P3). It introduces the key principles and practices of change management in the context of the latest research on key factors in successful change, as well as providing guidance on the appropriate application of different change management methodologies and highlighting available resources.

- For those directing or sponsoring change, it offers an overview of the key aspects of change management they should consider as part of their role (sections 3 and 6).
- For programme and project managers directly managing change programmes and projects, it provides an accessible introduction to the change management discipline within a familiar context and a starting point for those who have little background in the field (sections 2–7).
- For project professionals working in a change management environment, it helps raise awareness of the language and concepts involved (sections 2–3).
- For experienced change practitioners it provides a vehicle to help open dialogue and obtain buy-in from sponsors and project managers who may be less familiar with change management (section 4).

---

[1] In this context 'change' does not mean change control or IT change management. This is explained more fully in Section 3.1.

2

Introduction

All projects and programmes are ultimately created to deliver change of one form or another. Whether it be delivery of a new asset, process, structure or system, until it has actually been adopted and is used in the way it was intended, the change is not complete and the full benefits will not be realised. A recent Change Pulse survey (APM, 2016) indicated that over 90 per cent of organisations have had planned and managed change within the last three years. Key drivers of this change include strategic direction, new products and services, technology, regulatory requirements and the need to deliver efficiencies. Yet there are many well-publicised examples where change has not been successfully delivered and similar challenges can be found in almost any organisation. Research findings have not always been consistent but often demonstrate that the majority of projects and programmes do not fully succeed in achieving what they set out to do (see section 7.2). This is illustrated by the following diagram:

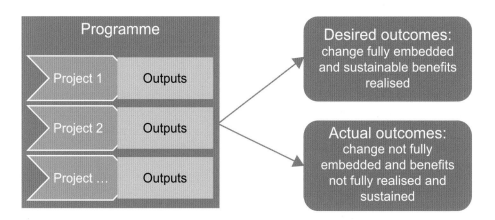

Change management is an evolving discipline which has developed significantly over the last 20 years. It recognises the specific challenges to implementing and embedding change and addresses these through leading, engaging and supporting people through change at both the individual and organisational levels. Managing change well can help address resistance and reduce performance impacts and secure sustainable benefits more rapidly.

Drawing on fields such as HR and psychology and recognising the innate variability and emotional nature of human response, change management does not always sit comfortably with the more formal technical processes of project and programme management. However, at its heart is a series of approaches which when applied appropriately will significantly increase the chances of successful adoption and embedding of change affecting people and culture, processes, organisations or technology. Fundamentally, it is about delivering change in a way which works with the people involved and brings them along on the journey, rather than simply presenting them with a *fait accompli* and expecting them to accept it. It is 'working with' rather than 'doing to'.

Managing change effectively requires much more than the technical P3 disciplines. When approached in a structured yet flexible manner, change management activities can be effectively integrated with other project or programme activities and contribute significantly to success, increasing sustainability and minimising any negative impact on business performance. In fact some programme management methodologies[2] explicitly recognise the importance of change management (or 'business change') in converting installed project outputs into programme outcomes which are fully implemented and embedded with the people involved. It is only then that the benefits can be fully realised. Change management should therefore be seen as a critical requirement for project and programme success.

Depending on the nature and scale of change involved, project professionals may find themselves directly undertaking change management activities where they have the capacity and appropriate skills. Alternatively, they may need to draw on specialist resources to help manage and facilitate change management (much as they call on engineering or technical specialists to fulfil their roles within the project team). Either way it is essential that project professionals have sufficient awareness and understanding of change management to recognise its importance in successfully managing change and be able to plan appropriately to undertake it. This publication is therefore intended to make change management relevant and accessible to project professionals.

It is also important to recognise that however well planned and executed projects or programmes may be, events will always occur which mean change emerges in ways that hadn't been intended or envisaged. Often this is most apparent in organisations which are more innovative or dynamic, or those particularly susceptible to external influences. Yet all organisations need to be

---

[2] Such as Managing Successful Programmes® (MSP, 2011).

ready to respond to emergent change. The principles introduced in this guide are equally applicable to change which is unplanned and unexpected, albeit that they may need to be deployed more rapidly and with less formal planning than in a more structured P3 environment.

This publication begins by defining and providing an overview of the change management discipline. It then goes on to explain in more detail the relationship between change management and project, programme and portfolio management and their complementary roles in the overall management of change. There are many different change management methodologies, developed in both academic and commercial environments. Whilst many of these draw on similar principles, it is recognised that this landscape may appear daunting to those new to change management, so the guide includes a section to help understand these and consider which may be most appropriate for different situations. Given that change management is still maturing as a discipline, new research is regularly giving greater insights into the aspects of change management which are most important for success and the next section of the guide covers these. This is followed by consideration of how to measure the success of change – and hence demonstrate the value that change management brings. Finally, the publication summarises further resources and references for additional reading, including the excellent range of material on the APM Enabling Change SIG's webpages.

Given the nature of this guide, it is important to note that whilst the principles and approaches covered provide a good introduction to the subject, the reality of change is often very complex. With a large number of individual perceptions, opinions and reactions to change, the effects can be difficult to predict and there are rarely easy solutions. Yet there is a need to start somewhere and it is envisaged this publication can contribute to building understanding as a step towards improving the 'real world' experience.

3

What is change management?

3.1 Context

The context for this publication is organisation and business change. This includes process, IT enabling and other forms of change. Change management in this context does **not** specifically relate to the following:

- IT change management in relation to the Information Technology Infrastructure Library (ITIL), a set of practices for IT service management.
- Change control of scope or milestones in project management.
- Change control within quality management systems (QMS) and information technology (IT) systems, which is a formal process used to ensure that changes to a product or system are introduced in a controlled and co-ordinated manner.

3.2 *APM Body of Knowledge* definition

The current *APM Body of Knowledge* refers to change management and defines it thus:

> Change management is a structured approach to moving an organisation from the current state to the desired future state.
>
> The conversion of project outputs into outcomes and benefits invariably requires some form of organisational change. Change involves both practical and psychological factors, so managing change in a structured and controlled manner is essential if the benefits in a business case are to be realised.
>
> A typical, generic, change management process might include the following steps, each of which resonates with the P3 environment and processes:

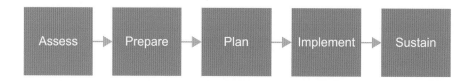

In P3 management the assess step constitutes identifying what is needed to translate desired outputs into clearly articulated outcomes and benefits. The prepare step involves creating a vision and gaining support. This is when stakeholder management is used to gain support for the outline business case, with particular emphasis on changes required for business-as-usual. This would also include establishing governance and roles to support change, such as the appointment of business change managers.

The plan step is a familiar process to both P3 managers and change managers. The various P3 plans and schedules must take change into account, particularly in the communication management plan and the risk management plan. The implement step is the heart of the process. It includes communicating the benefits of the change, removing obstacles and coordinating the activities that transform business-as-usual from the status quo to the new way of working.

For changes to deliver the benefits required by the business case, they have to be stable and become the normal way of working. The sustain step will continue beyond the P3 life cycle to ensure that value is continually realised from the investment in the project, programme or portfolio.

It is important to note that change management is defined differently by other organisations and authors. As a result of completing this *Introduction to Managing Change* the SIG has developed a new definition as a conclusion on page 41.

3.3 Change models and methodologies

There are a wide range of models and methodologies for managing change. The APM Enabling Change SIG webpages fully documents the group's current understanding of these. Although the SIG does not promote or recommend any particular methodology, this section introduces two well-known change models from John Kotter and Kurt Lewin by way of illustration.

3.4 John Kotter

In 1996 John Kotter wrote *Leading Change* (Kotter, 1996), which looked at what people did to transform their organisations. Kotter (1995) introduced an eight-step change model for helping managers deal with transformational change, which fundamentally alters the way the business operates. This is summarised below:

Kotter's approach has a number of factors in common with other models, like creating a clear vision, conducting good communication regarding the new vision, empowering employees, leading by example and celebrating successes. It is important to consider which change management model suits you best and adopt it in a logical and pragmatic fashion for your circumstances.

In the final analysis, Kotter believes that change sticks when it becomes 'the way we do things around here' when it seeps into the bloodstream of the corporate body. Until new behaviours are rooted in social norms and shared values, they are subject to degradation as soon as the pressure for change is removed. Change management is needed until it becomes intuitive. Ultimately everyone needs to do something differently in order for change to be successful, not change managers alone.

For *The Heart of Change* (2002) Kotter worked with Dan Cohen to look into the core problems people face when leading change. They concluded that the central issue was changing the behaviour of people and that successful change occurs when speaking to people's feelings. In other words people are much more likely to change their behaviour when they feel an emotional response which makes them want to change.

3.5 Kurt Lewin

Kurt Lewin emigrated from Germany to America during the 1930s and is recognised as the 'founder of social psychology', which highlights his interest in the human aspect of change.

His three-stage theory of change is commonly referred to as **Unfreeze, Change, Freeze** (or Refreeze) (Lewin, 1947). A lot has changed since the theory was originally presented in 1947, but the Kurt Lewin model is still extremely relevant and is illustrated below:

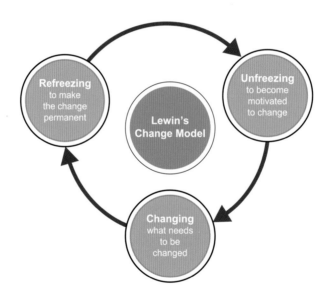

3.5.1 Stage 1: Unfreezing

The Unfreezing stage is probably one of the more important stages to understand in the world of change we live in today. This stage is about getting ready to change. It involves getting to a point of understanding that change is necessary and getting ready to move away from our current comfort zone. This first stage is about preparing ourselves, or others, before the change (and ideally creating a situation in which we want the change).

3.5.2 Stage 2: Change – or transition

Kurt Lewin was aware that change is not an event but rather a process and called that process a transition. Transition is the inner movement or journey we make in reaction to a change. This second stage occurs as we make the changes that are needed; people are 'unfrozen' and moving towards a new way of being.

3.5.3 Stage 3: Freezing (or refreezing)

Kurt Lewin refers to this stage as freezing, although it has also been referred to as 'refreezing'. As the name suggests, this stage is about establishing stability once the changes have been made. The changes are accepted and become the new norm. People form new relationships and become comfortable with their routines.

3.5.4 What does Kurt Lewin mean by 'freeze'?

In today's world of change, the next new change could happen in much shorter timescales. This rigidity of freezing does not fit with modern thinking about change being a continuous, sometimes chaotic process in which great flexibility is demanded.

Lewin's concern is about reinforcing the change and ensuring that the desired change is accepted and maintained into the future. Without this, people tend to go back to doing what they are used to doing.

4

The relationship between P3 and managing change

4.1 Introduction

Project management is familiar as both an established and evolving profession in itself and also as a specific competency or skillset within general management. This will probably be the case regardless of business sector or professional background. Organisations aren't as familiar with the specialism of change management, so in order to manage change it seems reasonable to ask how change management relates to project management, or to related activities like programme or portfolio management? Other questions follow on from this. Where does change management fit into the P3 hierarchy in an organisation and does it have a distinct role within an organisation's project environment?

4.2 Managing change

An organisation can have any number of projects that seek to deliver change of one form or another. They may begin as a bright idea, as a reaction to circumstances and market changes, or as an initiative related to the organisation's vision and objectives. Projects will have a beginning, middle and end, aligned to a particular timeline, budget and outputs, providing tangible deliverables measured by performance indicators and metrics related to time, cost and quality. Programmes will be made up of interrelated changes delivered through a number of projects requiring oversight to enable the delivery of wider outcomes and longer-term benefits.

An organisation's overarching portfolio will be made up of the different projects and programmes being delivered, managed together with business-as-usual (BAU) activities to deliver a particular business strategy or any number of goals. The distinction between BAU and P3 is that an organisation's BAU activities are running the business whereas its programmes and projects are changing the business. The alignment of the overall portfolio with business strategy will be a critical success factor that determines positive project outputs and programme outcomes, leading to business benefits and, over time, a virtuous circle of growth. However, the skills and disciplines of project, programme or portfolio management cannot in themselves guarantee full, sustainable achievement of the desired change. The management of change must be considered holistically, with P3 being viewed as a part of this rather than as the only lens through which all change is viewed. P3 should be seen as a delivery mechanism which contributes to managing change, rather than the complete solution. It can then be observed that change management is another important contributor to successfully delivering change, which works alongside and in tandem with P3.

Management at each level, be that the project, programme or portfolio, will require different roles and skills; this is the same for change management. The one thing in common is that they all have specialist skills and attributes that, harnessed together, can deliver successful, lasting and palpable organisational change.

4.3 Governance, accountability and the role of the PMO

Managing a portfolio of projects and programmes requires a defined governance hierarchy, creating lines of accountability and levels of authority that facilitate a reporting structure, which, in turn, supports decision-making and ensures that the portfolio remains aligned to the wider business strategy and organisational objectives. Given that this requires considerable coordination and collaboration, a PMO (portfolio management office or programme management office) may be created as a central management hub, to provide guidance on project methodologies, to ensure projects and programmes are regulatory compliant and to disseminate key information for executive reporting and decision-making.

The PMO, if carefully set up and resourced, has a crucial role in supporting the creation of controlled and manageable environments within an ever-moving organisational context. PMOs can be set up to support a variety of initiatives and there may be a central or corporate PMO that sits above these, sometimes called an 'enterprise' PMO. If an organisation wants to arrange its line management and reporting around its change initiatives, it may have a CMO, or change management office (Franklin, 2015). If this is the case, the distinction here will be, firstly, that this function is organisation-wide and thus able to manage change initiatives and dependencies which will have strategic, not localised, impacts and, secondly, that the CMO function will include staff from across the organisation who are influencing or affected by the changes planned, be they strategy managers, departmental heads or business leads affected by the changes. Responsibilities and accountabilities need to be thought through carefully and particular attention paid to the role of senior responsible owners and project or programme boards within the organisational structure.

4.4 Understanding how different P3 methodologies relate to change

The creation of the controlled environment that projects inhabit will separate them from the rest of the organisation's BAU activities. Nonetheless, there will be interaction by the project with the rest of the business through stakeholder engagement and communications, gathering key requirements, project design and business case approval at the very least. If a change manager is using a project or programme-based approach, consideration of the right methodology will be crucial from the outset. The selection of a project management method may be driven to some extent by industry norms (e.g. construction projects and the RIBA 2013 work stage model) but if projects are not driven by a particular industry norm or standard, there is a need to consider the options and choose a methodology carefully. Only general guidance is given here, but broadly, project methodologies can be broken down into two distinct types: waterfall and agile (see box over the page).

In either waterfall or agile approaches, change management activities must be integrated and it is important to consider what change management methodology integrates best with the project one. This is a constantly developing and evolving area as project managers and change practitioners explore ways and means to deliver projects and products ever more quickly in a demanding environment. There may be a requirement by the organisation to adhere to particular change methodologies, standards or tools as part of the transition, depending on its governance, the reporting and decision-making structure or the timelines involved. Clearly, change approaches in an agile environment will have to be adaptable; that is, they are able to handle evolving and unplanned for demands in a disciplined, robust and responsive way. The reference section on page 44 offers some helpful resources in this regard.

Waterfall methods are linear and sequential processes that follow a structured approach, whereby time and energy are directed towards the design stage and customer requirements are closely defined to avoid costly changes later on. Work will often be phased with stage gates that control expenditure and activity, which prohibit the movement of a project to the next stage until all conditions are met or when the decision to move forward is sanctioned by a governing body or board. As such this methodology is typically found in construction project environments and an example would be PRINCE2®.	*Agile methods* are iterative and incremental to allow business solutions to evolve in a flexible and interactive manner. The gradual development of prototypes, which add both components and complexity as an agile project progresses, will be more appropriate and potentially save time and money in fast-paced or uncertain contexts. Outputs will be delivered early in the process and tangible deliverables will occur quickly to allow for early feedback from the client or proof of concept from technical teams. This methodology is typically found in IT project environments such as DSDM.

4.5 Change leadership: managing change through a business change workstream

One common approach is to manage change through a specific project work-stream. Whilst this has the advantage of ensuring change management activities are explicitly recognised, it can have the effect of marginalising them rather than change management being integrated across the entire endeavour. If a change workstream approach is taken, the identification of a change management lead to support the project's delivery will be important for success. Change managers will need to develop the change workstream (or several, depending on the complexity and scope of change) that will plan and deliver the business change within BAU whilst aligned to the change plan. A change manager's role will be similar to the project manager's in that they will need to manage and report on their plan for the workstream, allocate specific activities within the workstream, use team resources effectively, provide vision and focus and also manage any risks, issues and dependencies. However, the change manager is the voice of change on the project and must ensure that business related change management activities are delivered.

4.6 Change leadership: managing all the relationships, interactions and interfaces

As a change manager, it is unlikely that a particular project or programme will be the only change initiative happening in the organisation. There is therefore a need to establish good relationships with other projects in order to carefully manage dependencies and avoid conflicts with them. It will be important to collaborate. Project and programme management tools and techniques, such as baselining and scheduling, building a target operating model or blueprint, establishing a critical path and working with the PMO can all help in understanding a changing context and creating the information flows required to enable the project to progress in relation to the rest of the business. Nevertheless, it is essential that technical structures and governance controls (the project) are complemented by change activities and stakeholder management (the people).

There may be distinct roles within the change team in that a project manager will deliver the outputs and deliverables against the project plan, whereas a change manager will work to ensure the organisation is able to accept and embed the change. While project reporting is likely to be hierarchical through to the portfolio level, business change reporting may be by function and will almost certainly involve a matrix management arrangement. The important point is that, if this is the case, respective project and change roles are clarified, so that activities are agreed and accountabilities are clear from the start and stakeholders are kept informed.

4.7 Change leadership: balancing the change project's needs with the organisation's expectations

It is paramount that change projects are aligned to the business strategy of the organisation. Stakeholder management is crucial, as a proliferation in the number of requirements will result in scope creep which will burden the projects, putting the delivery plan, resources, outcomes and benefits at risk. While identifying quick wins, an experienced change manager may want to phase or delay the full roll-out of a project if giving time to embed will result in a better outcome and a better realisation of its benefits. Indeed, some areas will be easier to transition than others, while others need to transition first for the rest to follow. Precise timelines will have to be robustly negotiated and customer expectations carefully managed for the change project to succeed. Business-critical activities will have to be protected to mitigate the risks during transition.

4.8 Managing transition: the return to business-as-usual and creating a 'new normal'

For a project to be successful, people will need to be led and supported through the change and people skills cannot be emphasised enough. A change network or community may be established to encourage positive behaviours and early adoption. There will need to be detailed work around communications plans for stakeholder engagement. Similarly, the change manager needs to ensure that detailed handovers are in place for the new roles that are starting and for passing on knowledge from existing roles too. Knowledge share and transfer will be critical, so that the knowledge held is retained and the knowledge base is widened. It is likely that a training budget will be required and that training requirements must be reviewed and prioritised appropriately across the teams.

Documenting transition activities is important, not only in terms of a target operating model or blueprint, but also to outline systems that will be used, key contractors or suppliers and high-level processes that will assist staff in their new roles. It is often necessary to have embedding activities in the BAU environment that sustain the change long after the project or programme in question is finished. Equally, it may be a while before the full business benefits are realised and these will need to be monitored and tracked to completion. Again, people skills and engagement with teams in BAU cannot be emphasised enough.

4.9 Change management and P3 management in perspective

Change management involves a varied and wide-ranging skillset which encompasses project management and people development in a challenging organisational context. However, an understanding of the different tools, processes and methodologies and their application, together with well-thought-out structures for reporting and decision-making based on a tried and tested project delivery model will make for a robust organisational approach that supports successful and lasting change. Whilst it is tempting to see a merging of roles between project and change management, or to argue for one over the other, it is probably best to see these as complementary parts of successful change delivery. They not only require different skillsets, but also different perspectives that will enrich both the projects developing within the organisation and the dialogue between different teams. This in turn will encourage a mature community to emerge of professionals skilled in best practice.

5

Overview of approaches to managing change

5.1 Introduction

The Greek philosopher Heraclitus said that "there is nothing permanent except change". Change is now occurring at an even greater pace, with the impact of technology accelerating this rate of change, and the challenge for today's leaders is to respond quickly and effectively to external and internal developments.

Constant change pressures organisations into the continued modification of what is the operational norm and the leadership needs to respond to the challenges of change to ensure organisational survival and progress.

Leaders are looking for ways to reduce the risk and failure levels of their organisations' change initiatives and using a structured, co-ordinated approach to change helps prepare for planned and unplanned changes. Different ways of managing change are termed methodologies, frameworks, models and approaches, and definitions of these are as follows:

Methodology – a system of methods used in a particular area of study or activity
Framework – a basic structure underlying a system, concept, or text
Model – a representation of a person or thing or of a proposed structure
Approach – a way of dealing with a situation or problem

5.2 Why use a change approach?

In Prosci's annual benchmarking studies participants have been asked about the greatest contributors to the success of their changes and applying a structured approach to change has remained a top contributor for over 10 years (Prosci, 2016):

17

- A structured approach has remained the second or third most important contributor to project success.
- In three of the last five change management best practices studies, the use of a structured approach to change management was cited as the second greatest contributor to success (behind only active and visible executive sponsorship). A structured approach to change moves organisations away from merely reacting to resistance to change and provides a solid framework for engaging and mobilising impacted employees.
- Nearly 80 per cent of study participants utilised a structured approach.
- The data in the 2013 study showed a continued growth in those participants following a particular change management methodology and the percentage of participants utilising a methodology more than doubled between 2003 (34 per cent) and 2013 (79 per cent).

However, the recent APM Change Pulse survey indicated that only around half of respondents were using a recognised formal change methodology (APM, 2016), suggesting that there is a significant opportunity for more organisations to benefit from using a structured approach.

5.3 Documented approaches to managing change

The APM Enabling Change SIG has documented 22 approaches to managing change, providing a description and overview, background and origins, typical uses, industry sector, how the approach differs from others and further information. A summary of these approaches is provided below:

5.3.1 The Association of Change Management Professionals (ACMP) Standard for Change Management

This is a collection of generally accepted practices in change management, released in September 2014. The Standard establishes five key change management areas that will enhance practice proficiency, quality and credibility across multiple industries, organisations and roles: 1. Evaluating change impact and organisational readiness; 2. Formulating change management strategy; 3. Developing change management plans; 4. Executing change management plans; and 5. Closing the change management effort.

5.3.2 The Accelerating Implementation Methodology (AIM)

This is a flexible, business-disciplined change management methodology for managing organisational changes including transformational change through to full return on investment. AIM can be applied to any kind of initiative or project. The AIM Roadmap depicts the ten-step change management methodology approach associated with planning, implementing and monitoring any change or initiative: 1. Define the change; 2. Build agent capacity; 3. Assess the climate; 4. Generate sponsorship; 5. Determine change approach; 6. Develop target readiness; 7. Build a communication plan; 8. Develop a reinforcement strategy; 9. Create cultural fit; and 10. Prioritise action.

5.3.3 CHAMPS2

This is a vision-led, benefits-driven business transformation method which is broad in scope and encompasses the whole business change journey. It helps define an organisation's strategic needs and then provides a tailored route to ensure that the desired outcomes are achieved. CHAMPS2 divides transformational change into eight phases: 1. Transformation initiation; 2. Visioning; 3. Shaping and planning; 4. Design; 5. Service creation and realisation; 6. Proving and transition; 7. Stabilisation; and 8. Benefits realisation.

5.3.4 e-change®

This is an Enterprise Change Management platform from Changefirst. The IT platform enables organisations to create, deploy and manage change programmes. They have their own change method – People Centred Implementation (PCI) – which underpins their platform and the training they provide. As it is Changefirst's in-house method it is not publicly available. The method hinges around six critical success factors: 1. Shared change purpose; 2. Effective change leadership; 3. Powerful engagement processes; 4. Committed local sponsors; 5. Strong personal connection; and 6. Sustained personal performance.

5.3.5 The Change Management Institute (CMI) Body of Knowledge

The CMI has developed a Body of Knowledge which covers a broad and useful spectrum of areas including: 1. Overarching theories behind change; 2. Defining change; 3. Managing benefits; 4. Stakeholder strategies; 5. Communication and engagement; 6. Change impact; 7. Change readiness, planning and measurement; 8. Project management; 9. Education, learning and support; 10. Facilitation; 11. Sustaining systems; 12. Personal and professional management; and 13. Organisational considerations.

The CMI has also created its own organisational change maturity model (OCMM) which is used to describe the behaviours, practices and processes of an organisation to enable reliable and sustainable outcomes.

5.3.6 The Change Execution Methodology (CEM)

Conner Partners focus on helping organisations achieve the expected value and intended outcomes of change and offer a framework built on decades of application history. The Change Execution Methodology (CEM) is designed to proactively identify and mitigate risks to realisation. CEM provides the steps to develop a plan, assign resources, estimate duration and anticipate and mitigate risk, while maintaining a line-of-sight to the promised outcomes.

5.3.7 The Change Leaders Roadmap (CLR)

This has been developed by BeingFirst, a specialist change leadership development and transformational change consulting firm. The roadmap describes how to navigate the complexities of organisational transformation. It uses a nine-phase approach to plan, design and implement major change efforts successfully. The nine phases are: 1. Prepare to lead the change; 2. Create organisational vision, commitment and capability; 3. Assess the situation to determine design requirements; 4. Design the desired state; 5. Analyse the impact; 6. Plan and organise for implementation; 7. Implement the change; 8. Celebrate and integrate the new state; and 9. Learn and course correct.

5.3.8 The Boston Consulting Group (BCG) Change Delta Framework

This framework was developed by BCG to support their clients in the delivery of change programmes. It was created to address two key determining factors of change success or failure, which, according to an Economic Intelligence Unit study, are clearly defined milestones that measure progress and the commitment of senior leadership. The framework consists of the following elements: 1. Governance and project management office; 2. Executional certainty; 3. Enabled leaders; and 4. Engaged organisation.

5.3.9 Bridges' Transition Model

This model by Williams Bridges focuses on the transition that people go through when faced with change. The main strength of the model is that it focuses on transition, not change. The model highlights three stages of transition that people go through when they experience change: 1. Ending, losing and letting go; 2. The neutral zone; and 3. The new beginning.

5.3.10 Kotter's Eight Steps

Dr John Kotter has been involved in change and leadership research for nearly 40 years. He identified and extracted the success factors and combined them into a methodology, the eight-step process: 1. Create a sense of urgency; 2. Build a guiding coalition; 3. Form a strategic vision and initiatives; 4. Enlist a volunteer army; 5. Enable action by removing barriers; 6. Generate short-term wins; 7. Sustain acceleration; and 8. Institutionalise change (see section 3.4).

5.3.11 The Change Curve

This is based on a model originally developed in the 1960s by Elisabeth Kübler-Ross to explain the grieving process. Since then it has been widely utilised as a method of helping people understand their reactions to significant change or upheaval. The original five stages of grief – denial, anger, bargaining, depression and acceptance – have been adapted over the years. There are numerous versions of the curve in existence. However, the majority of them are consistent in their use of the following basic emotions, which are often grouped into three distinct transitional stages: 1 – shock and denial; 2 – anger; 3 – bargaining; 4 – depression; 5 – acceptance.

5.3.12 Lewin's Three Stages of Change

One of the cornerstone models for understanding organisational change was developed by Kurt Lewin in the 1940s and 1950s and is still used today. His model is a simple and easy-to-understand framework for managing change known as Unfreeze – Change – Refreeze. Lewin, a physicist as well as social scientist, explained organisational change using the analogy of changing the shape of a block of ice, i.e. unfreezing a large cube of ice to change it and reform it into a cone of ice. By recognising these three distinct stages of change, it is possible to plan to implement the change required (see section 3.5).

5.3.13 Managing Successful Programmes® (MSP)

This represents proven programme management good practice in the successful delivery of transformational change through the application of programme management. The MSP framework is based on three core concepts: 1. MSP principles; 2. MSP governance themes; and 3. MSP transformational flow. This provides a route through the life cycle of a programme from its conception through to the delivery of the new capability, outcomes and benefits.

5.3.14 The Project Management Institute (PMI)'s Change Management Methodology

This is a change methodology that sits alongside PMI's project, programme and portfolio management processes to assist in "successfully designing, creating, implementing and sustaining organisational change". The method is encapsulated in the *Managing Change: A Practice Guide* publication.

5.3.15 Pritchett's Change Management Model

Pritchett is a training and consultancy organisation specialising in change management and merger integration. Pritchett's model provides a simple phased approach for managing both the project and people sides of change initiatives. The methodology consists of four phases: 1. Imperative; 2. Readiness; 3. Implementation; and 4. Gain. Action is taken to ensure that the future change initiatives capitalise on previous gains and insights.

5.3.16 The Prosci ADKAR Model

This is central to the change management work the Prosci organisation supports. ADKAR stands for: Awareness of the need for change; Desire to participate and support the change; Knowledge on how to change; Ability to implement required skills and behaviours; Reinforcement to sustain the change.

5.3.17 The Viral Change™ Journey

Viral Change™ works on the basis of using the power of a small set of well-defined non-negotiable behaviours, spread by small groups of highly connected individuals within the organisation. The journey is divided into five phases, although not all of them are as sequential as represented. The duration of each phase varies depending on where the change process starts. The five phases are: 1. Discovery; 2. Development; 3. Engagement; 4. Diffusion; and 5. Sustain.

5.3.18 The Managed Change™ Approach

This delivers change management through LaMarsh Global's Managed Change™ Model and Methodology. Driven by real data, LaMarsh Global's proprietary change management approach guides project teams, change agents and sponsors and focuses on the people side to accurately identify and reduce employee resistance to change. The methodology is organised as a roadmap consisting of the following stages: 1. Identify the change; 2. Prepare the change; 3. Plan the change; 4. Implement the change; and 5. Sustain the change.

5.3.19 Senge Learning Organisations

A learning organisation is one that 'learns' and encourages learning among its people. By promoting the exchange of information between employees it creates a more knowledgeable workforce and a more flexible organisation where people will accept and adapt to new ideas and change through shared vision.

Popularised by Peter Senge in 1990, what distinguishes learning organisations from more traditional organisations is the mastery of five basic disciplines: 1. Systems thinking; 2. Personal mastery; 3. Mental models; 4. Building shared vision; and 5. Team learning.

5.3.20 McKinsey 7-S Model

The basic premise of the 7-S Model is that there are seven internal aspects of an organisation that need to be aligned if it is to be successful. These seven inter-dependent factors (where a change in one affects all the others) are categorised as either 'hard' or 'soft' elements: 1. Strategy: the plan devised to maintain and build competitive advantage over the competition; 2. Structure: the way the organisation is structured and who reports to whom; 3. Systems: the daily activities and procedures that staff members engage in to get the job done; 4. Shared values: the core values of the company that are evidenced in the corporate culture and the general work ethic; 5. Style: the style of leadership adopted; 6. Staff: the employees and their general capabilities; and 7. Skills: the actual skills and competencies of the employees working for the company. Some organisations have adopted an 'extended' model with two additional elements: Surroundings and Sustainability.

5.3.21 Lewin Force-field Analysis

Force-field analysis is an influential development in social science. It provides a framework for looking at the factors (*forces*) that influence a situation, originally social situations. It looks at forces that are either driving movement towards a goal (helping forces) or blocking movement towards a goal (hindering forces). The principle, developed by Kurt Lewin, is a significant contribution to the fields of social science, psychology, organisational development, process management and change management.

5.3.22 Change Equation

The formula for change was created by David Gleicher while he was working at Arthur D. Little in the early 1960s and refined by Kathie Dannemiller in the 1980s. This formula provides a model to assess the relative strengths affecting the likely success of organisational change programmes.

The original formula, as created by Gleicher and published by Beckhard, is:

$$C = (ABD) > X$$

where: **C** = change; **A** = the status quo dissatisfaction; **B** = a desired clear state; **D** = practical steps to the desired state; **X** = the cost of the change.

It was Kathleen Dannemiller who dusted off the formula and simplified it, making it more accessible for consultants and managers. Dannemiller and Jacobs first published the more common version of the formula in 1992. Paula Griffin stated that Gleicher started it, Beckhard and Harris promoted it, but it really took off when Dannemiller changed the language to make it easier to remember and use.

$$\text{Dannemiller version: } D \times V \times F > R$$

Three factors must be present for meaningful organisational change to take place. These factors are: **D** = Dissatisfaction with how things are now; **V** = Vision of what is possible; **F** = First, concrete steps that can be taken towards the vision.

If the product of these three factors is greater than **R** = Resistance then change is possible. Because D, V and F are multiplied, if any one is absent (zero) or low, then the product will be zero or low and therefore not capable of overcoming the resistance.

Further details of all these approaches to managing change are available in the APM Enabling Change SIG's Change Methods Library document on the APM website.

6

Key factors in successful change

There are some key factors in successful change, irrespective of the sector involved, or the nature of the change.

6.1 Examples from the literature

Examples of published sources include Andrea Shapiro's *Creating Contagious Commitment* (Shapiro, 2003) and her 'seven levers of change'. For her, the biggest drivers of success are the level of contact between 'advocates' and 'apathetics', having an effective infrastructure in place to support the change and sponsors 'walking the talk'. Other drivers include 'mass exposure' (effective communication), 'hiring advocates' (the champions for the change), finding ways to 'shift resistance' and using reward and recognition mechanisms.

A Global McKinsey Survey (2000) demonstrated that the greater the level of staff contribution and involvement in change, the more successful the outcome.

Loveland (2012), cited in *The Effective Change Manager's Handbook* (2014: 51) states that, 'Continuing research by Prosci with 650 participants from 62 countries identified the greatest contributor to overall change management success as "active and visible executive sponsorship". The greatest obstacle was said by the respondents to be "ineffective change management sponsorship from senior leaders".'

Prosci's (2016) research covering 1,120 change leaders ranked the greatest contributors to success as follows:

1. Active and visible sponsorship.
2. Structured change management approach.
3. Dedicated change management resources.
4. Integration with project management.
5. Employee engagement and participation.
6. Frequent and open communication.
7. Engagement with middle managers.

The 'People Centred Implementation' model (Changefirst, 2016) includes six 'critical success factors' for successful change:

1. Shared change purpose.
2. Effective change leadership.
3. Powerful engagement processes.
4. Committed local sponsors.
5. Strong personal connection.
6. Sustained personal performance.

The list used in this publication, and the descriptions, have been developed from the collective experience and expertise of the authors, input from P3 and change practitioners during SIG and APM branch events, the recent Change Pulse survey (APM, 2016) and learning from the literature.

6.2 Working list of key factors for successful change

The key factors can be broadly grouped under the following headings:

1. Formulate a clear vision and strategy, supported by well-defined benefits.
2. Ensure strong leadership and sponsorship.
3. Define and follow a well-structured and integrated approach.
4. Understand, engage with, build commitment from and support key stakeholders.
5. Build a strong change team with the necessary capabilities for success.
6. Measure the success of the change initiative.

Respondents to the Change Pulse survey (APM, 2016) indicated that the two most important factors in their organisations were clear vision and strategy and strong leadership and sponsorship, with engagement also a high priority.

6.2.1 Formulate a clear vision and strategy, supported by well-defined benefits

People are more likely to accept change if they understand why it is happening, what it will entail and how it will affect them. Individual change projects and programmes must be aligned with the overall strategy of the business and co-ordinated to create a manageable 'picture' of change. Define the vision clearly and concisely, tailored in a way that will communicate the 'WIIFM' (what's in it for me) for each individual within the organisation. Take a bottom-up as well as a top-down approach, involving people in the definition of the vision. Articulate the drivers for change (why it is happening) and talk about outcomes. Use visuals to help convey the vision and make it memorable. Ensure people understand how the vision differs from business-as-usual ('to be' versus 'as is' state). Keep the vision under review to ensure it is still valid.

Well-defined benefits provide something tangible for people to understand, aim for and ultimately measure in terms of how well the benefits have been realised.

There are a number of tools and techniques that can help with the definition of visions, such as understanding the environment (for example using the PESTLE model (political, economic, sociological, technical, legal, ecological)), SWOT (strengths, weaknesses, opportunities, threats) analysis, force-field analysis and elevator pitches. Making a compelling case for change is sometimes described as a 'burning platform' from which there is no alternative but to move in order to survive, even if the alternative is uncertain or even dangerous (Conner, 1992, 2012).

Guidance on defining business cases and developing benefits realisation plans are available in PRINCE2®, in the *APM Body of Knowledge* and from other organisations. There is also a Harvard Business Review Guide on developing your business case (Sheen and Gallo, 2015).

Other relevant references include Collins and Porras (1994), MSP (2011), Kotter (1996), Bridges (1991) and Cap Gemini (2016).

6.2.2 Ensure strong leadership and sponsorship

Actions speak louder than words. It is important that guidance and support are provided to senior managers and sponsors so that they not only advocate but act as role models for the change. Involve all the right people from the organisation to drive and support the change so that there is real ownership from the business. Ensure sponsors have the necessary sphere of influence, the time available and the attributes to deliver, i.e. communication and listening skills, integrity, the ability to engage and inspire, trust, emotional intelligence and gravitas. Continuity of sponsorship is the ideal to strive for and, failing that, succession planning.

Sponsor terms of reference will help, along with competency frameworks, coaching and suggested content for communications. Psychometric tools and 360-degree feedback may also help to understand and develop effective leaders and sponsors.

It is also important to have feedback mechanisms in place. Make sure that there are rewards and recognition as well as escalation procedures to support the work of the change team and apply them if necessary.

Other relevant references and tools include Action Centred Leadership (Adair, 1988), Situational Leadership (Blanchard and Hersey, 1988), Prosci sponsor assessment and agile gate reviews.

6.2.3 Define and follow a well-structured and integrated approach

Adopt one of the many well-documented change methodologies and standards (see section 5), combined with strong programme and project management. Choose one that integrates well with what you already have in place in your organisation and make sure that you collect, share, review and act on lessons learned.

Be flexible in your approach to match the nature of the change programme and make the programme and its roadmap visible to your stakeholders. Have regular review and feedback loops. Remember the methodology in times of crisis and remember to think about delivery as well as just methodology.

Manage programme/project interdependencies across the whole organisation in a way that optimises your change programme. Avoid a silo mentality.

Ensure that you plan for final embedding of the change, so that it does become a way of working. Only then will the anticipated benefits finally be realised (Goodman, 2013). Refer to illustration over page.

Design and deliver communication, training and support interventions that achieve what they are meant to achieve, for all the different stakeholders involved. Communicate, communicate and communicate. Consider a wide range of creative communication approaches, with priority given to face-to-face contact.

Have everyone in the change team, the wider programme or project team and sponsors 'singing from the same hymn sheet', so that all messages are consistent and reinforce each other.

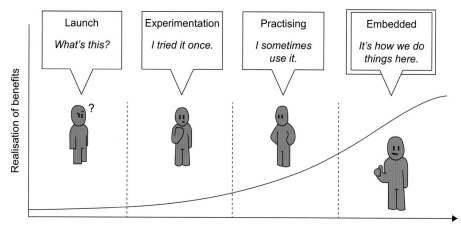

6.2.4 Understand, engage with, build commitment from and support all stakeholders

Each stakeholder and group of stakeholders will perceive and respond to the change differently. Review the change methodologies and standards for tools that will help you to understand, engage with, build commitment from and support stakeholders.

Develop a stakeholder management plan, carrying out the analysis to do so early in the change programme. Make sure you have all of your stakeholders identified, at every level of the organisation. Assess what the impact will be on these stakeholders and how you will manage it, as part of developing your plan. Revisit that impact during and at the end of the programme.

Engage with and nurture your stakeholders to build trust, so that they want to help you make the change succeed and feel supported through it (win hearts and minds). Work with key influencers. Use senior stakeholders as champions.

Spend time to really understand stakeholders – their perspectives and motivations. Ensure two-way communication, talk the stakeholders' language, seek feedback, listen, build relationships and trust. Communication alone does not guarantee engagement.

Consider the psychology and behaviours of change and pitch the timing of interactions at the point where they will have the most impact (neither too early nor too late). Be aware, when working in collaboration or partnership with other organisations, of the added complexity involved in these stakeholders' own organisations.

Take account of all the other changes and work pressures affecting stakeholders so as to make the whole experience as positive and painless for them as possible.

6.2.5 Build a strong change team with the necessary capabilities for success

Nurture your team to make it a high-performance unit that combines a clear focus on its task with strong interpersonal relationships. Make sure that the purpose or remit of the team is well defined in its own right and in relation to other teams, including the overall programme or project team.

Ensure that you have the right people in the team, that it is diverse and multi-disciplinary, that roles and responsibilities are well defined and that there are recognition and reward mechanisms in place. Understand people's motivations within the team and consider using psychometric tools[3] to help develop under-standing and ensure that you play to people's strengths. It helps if team members have strong relationships with stakeholders, communicate well and have a passion and energy for their remit.

Have team-building events and the right mix and frequency of team meetings to progress and support the team's work. Models such as Tuckman's Stages of Team Development can be helpful as a tool to help understand the dynamics within the change team. Equip team members with the necessary change process and soft/people capabilities or skills to enable successful change. Develop and support change agents, advocates and champions, whether formal members of your team or representatives in the stakeholder community.

If working with third parties, explore ways to achieve high performance within their teams and in their interactions with your team.

---

[3] Common psychometric tools for development and team building include Colourworks/Insights, Belbin, Myers-Briggs Type Indicator (MBTI) and StrengthFinder.

6.2.6 Measure the success of the change initiative

Test or pilot and monitor your change initiative so that you can adjust your approach as needed, demonstrate success, learn from experience and build and share success stories. Make sure you have a baseline and success criteria at the outset and relate measures to the originally defined vision and benefits. Section 7 describes approaches to measuring the success of change. Recognise that it may take time, beyond the formal closure of the change programme, to have a full set of measures of the outcome.

7

How do we measure change success?

"What gets measured gets improved"

Peter F. Drucker

7.1 Introduction

Measuring the success of a change initiative is the first step in understanding if it is on the right path or not and if adjustments are required to the plan activating these as necessary. It also demonstrates to senior executives, sponsors and wider stakeholders how the change initiative is delivering the original objectives and whether the deployed resources are sufficient or not.

Organisational change is often a non-linear, evolutionary discovery process and it is not possible to know absolutely everything at the beginning. The external and internal organisational environment can change during the process, and it is very difficult and even unrealistic to evaluate an organisational change initiative in the same way as other aspects of the business such as operations.

According to a recent Change Pulse survey, 38 per cent of the respondents didn't agree any success criteria for the change initiative as part of programme/ project set-up and initial planning (APM, 2016). This shows there is still a gap in how measurement of change success is set out at the onset.

Measures can also be excellent tools for engaging and communicating with the wider organisation and stakeholders on the effectiveness and impact of the change over time, and to seek feedback.

According to Davey (2012), measurement and evaluation of organisation change success is an extremely complex, difficult process carrying the risk of exposing failure. It is also an emotional, highly politicised process but can add credibility and augment organisational learning. It is therefore very important to plan and decide how the measurement should take place in a way that is acceptable to the stakeholders.

7.2 Background

The rates of success and failure for organisational change are a much-debated topic. Various figures have been quoted by research studies and journal papers, for example:

- Only 55 per cent of change projects are initially successful and only one in four are successful in the long run (Towers Watson, 2013).
- Only 56 per cent of change initiatives are successful (Economist, 2011).
- 41 per cent of projects were considered successful in meeting project objectives; the remaining 59 per cent missed at least one objective or failed completely (IBM, 2008).
- Only a third of the organisations are successful in managing change (McKinsey, 2008).
- 70 per cent of all change initiatives fail (Kotter, 2008; Beer and Nohria, 2000).

Hughes (2011) in his seminal journal paper offered a very critical view on these quoted failure rates, carried out a review of the journals and studies at the time and found no valid and reliable empirical evidence, raising numerous questions about the origins.

Other issues found with success/failure rate statistics were as follows:

a. Varying definition of change, project and programmes found in academia, practice and from one organisation to another.
b. Definition of 'success' – would failure to achieve one or more objectives of an organisational change initiative be a complete failure or partial failure?
c. Timing of 'success' measurement – was it done before, during and at the end of the change initiative?
d. Ambiguity around measures of success/failure – measures differ depending on the nature of organisational change and between different industries as well as organisations. Within organisations different change initiatives could be measured in different ways.
e. Success/failure measured from different perspectives of senior executives, shareholders, managers, employees, supply chain partners and those impacted by the change often varies.
f. Psychological biases and judgement errors play a role in baselining current performance, establishing measures, setting success criteria and applying measurement techniques.

7.3 Factors to consider

The diagram below shows some of the key factors that should be considered when measuring the success of any change initiative. These are explained further in the following paragraphs.

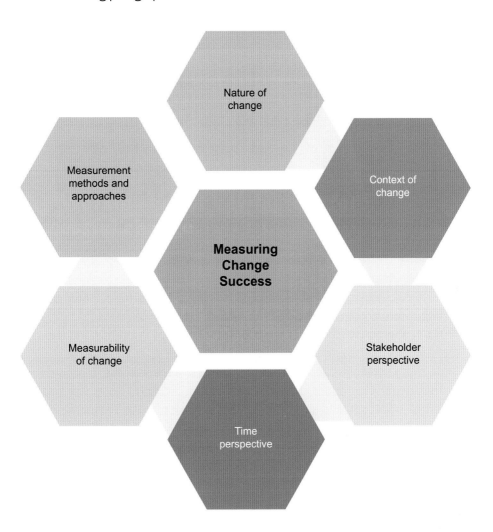

7.3.1 Nature of change

▪ Original stated goals and objectives – which are highly influenced by the culture within the organisation.

- Recognise and factor in continuous improvement throughout the change life cycle.
- Dynamic nature of change – anticipated and unanticipated outputs, outcomes and benefits.

7.3.2 Context of change

- Organisation-wide and/or industry-sector-specific challenges.
- Different types and drivers for change.
- Challenges across different countries and cultures.
- Ever-changing internal and external environment of the organisation.
- Dependency on other change initiatives – be they internal or external to the organisation.

7.3.3 Stakeholder perspective

- Measure success of your change initiative from the viewpoint of different stakeholders:
  - □ Internal – employees, managers, senior executives, sponsors and change delivery teams.
  - □ External – customers, shareholders, supply chain partners, communities, regulatory bodies and local authorities.
- Build in appropriate feedback mechanisms and loops – internal and external perceptions can be competing.
- Individuals maintain their own perception of change success in accordance with their personal values and beliefs.
- Informal judgement and evaluation will always take place as a result, no matter how defined the success measure might be.
- Understanding and measuring 'change experience' of stakeholders has the potential to be a powerful tool for monitoring and making adjustments for a successful transition.

7.3.4 Time perspective

According to Lewin (1947), we use measures against the background of time to assess change – the rate, extent and impact – and to establish the opposite of change stability.

- It is really important to recognise the change time continuum. The delivery is temporary in nature; however, the sustainability and stickiness of change extends far beyond.
- Past history of success and/or failure within the organisation or even industry sectors.

7.3.5 Measurability of change

Looking at the typical change lifecycle in section 3.2, overall a change initiative can be summarised in terms of outputs produced, outcomes achieved and benefits realised. Equally important is to consider how the effectiveness of the change management process will be measured for improvement and learning. This helps in building change capability and a higher level of organisational change maturity for future initiatives.

It is therefore valuable to consider measures across these three different elements:

- Output based:
  - Projects produce outputs which are important to achieve outcomes. According to a report published by APM (2014), measures for a successful project were time, budget, specification and quality, funder's satisfaction, stakeholder's satisfaction and overall project.
- Outcome based:
  - Change effectiveness and impact (leadership, sponsorship, adoption, resistance/readiness, attitudes, behaviours, knowledge, awareness).
  - Consideration for outcome-based measures is often a real oversight in the change success measures. Often the discussions focus on either just the outputs, benefit realisation or a combination of both.
- Benefits:
  - Measurable improvement in performance (return on investment, revenue, costs, compliance, other key performance indicators).
  - It is a rare change initiative where benefits realisation can be measured immediately after going live. Benefits often take some time to start to become apparent. This can be because it takes time for new habits to form with behavioural change, for proficiency to increase with systems/application usage, or for business cycles to play out.
  - Understand disbenefits (what stakeholders give up) and choose appropriate methodology to measure the impact.

7.3.6 Measurement methods and approaches

Depending on the nature and context of a change initiative, a variety of measurement methods and approaches can be used. This will also differ from one organisation to another and is quite often dictated by stakeholder requirements (for example regulatory bodies).

Broadly speaking they are divided into qualitative and quantitative measures and as explained in section 7.3.5 above should include outputs, outcome and benefit-based elements.

Qualitative measures are often gathered using approaches such as feedback surveys (online or in person), focus groups, interviews, observation and questioning techniques. This data/information collected over time can then be used to evaluate trends and performance in before, during and after states. It is, however, important to remember the inherent subjectivity in the nature of quantitative measures.

Quantitative measures rely on data and information which can be either generated electronically via a software/application or collected manually. Quantitative measures lend themselves really well to analysis of trends and performance over time through the before, during and after states.

This, however, doesn't mean that one measure is better than the other or it is a binary choice between quantitative and qualitative. The choice would really be influenced by the key factors explained in section 7.3.

Some of the more common measurement approaches are summarised in the following table:

Benefit realisation	Balanced scorecard
Service level agreements (SLAs)	Critical success factors/key performance indicators
Employee engagement/perception surveys	European Foundation for Quality Management Model
Focus groups	HM Treasury Green Book (five-case model)
Exit interviews	Agile/incremental delivery measures
Change readiness/resistance measures	Culture/leadership measures
Financial performance measures	Customer satisfaction/perception surveys
Time-based measures	Health, safety, quality and environmental measures
Knowledge, skills and attitudinal measures	Statistical analysis and measures

Other important factors to consider and pitfalls to avoid when it comes to measurability are:

1. **Vital few versus trivial many** – it provides focus to the evaluation exercise and reduces resource requirements. Ensure measures are relevant to the change initiative and remember the context of the wider organisation and linkages.
2. **Focus on the measures that stakeholders value** – others may help but may not be relevant for the stakeholders. Consider a balanced mixture of hard and soft, leading and lagging performance measures, a distinction that is often not understood and is therefore missed.
3. **Be clear on how long key performance indicators (KPIs) will be measured for** – not all outcomes will be achieved straight away and most benefits are realised months or even years after implementation.
4. **Gain agreement on what data will be tracked by whom** throughout the change lifecycle. The data and the resources to collect may not exist. Be clear on roles and responsibilities as this will increase the likelihood that the measures will be tracked well and people will be rewarded for doing so. Also bear in mind the repeatability and reliability of the data/information collected.
5. **Gain commitment from key stakeholders to review performance results** – what gets reviewed gets measured. This will ensure measuring change is not a wasted effort and can be used as a fantastic tool for engagement, communication and continuous improvement.
6. **Gather anecdotal feedback from people who are working with the changes** – verbatim comments, user stories or visuals help better describe benefits and lessons learned.
7. **Use tracked results to support business cases for future change initiatives** – this is often a missed opportunity.
8. **Communicate results to the stakeholders** – this increases engagement and invites people to celebrate success and learn from mistakes.
9. **Baseline current performance and determine new performance after delivery** – a clear baseline is needed at the outset but be prepared to flex and adapt as necessary.
10. **Create a 'test and learn' process** – to ensure that the change initiative drives the desired impact you can adjust your approach as needed, demonstrate success and learn from experience.

8

Conclusion: considerations for choosing an approach to managing change

8.1 Key factors in selecting a change approach

The APM Enabling Change SIG is agnostic in terms of recommending an approach to managing change but there are key factors to consider in selecting a specific approach. The approach should:

- be overarching and holistic;
- be integrated with the organisation strategy;
- be practical to deploy;
- be understandable and not too technical in language;
- be structured;
- identify change success factors and benefits;
- be communicated throughout the organisation;
- take into consideration the culture of the organisation; and
- consider the scale and type of change.

The APM Enabling Change SIG recommends an overarching, holistic approach to managing change, to deliver strategic objectives in a structured and co-ordinated way, illustrated over the page:

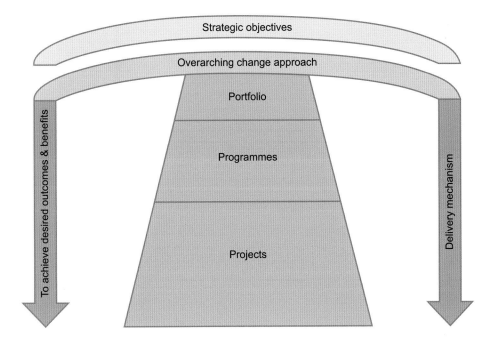

8.2 APM Enabling Change SIG proposed definition of managing change

Managing change is an overarching, holistic approach for implementing strategic and operational change in an organisation using a co-ordinated, structured and practical method working with all stakeholders to achieve the intended outcomes and benefits.

9

Resources

The APM website contains a number of additional resources on managing change and P3 management that you may find useful.

Stakeholder engagement

A vital part of managing change is engaging and working with stakeholders. The APM People SIG have more information on this at apm.org.uk/resources/find-a-resource/stakeholder-engagement.

Community

The APM Enabling Change SIG can be found at the following address: apm.org.uk/community/enabling-change-sig

Publications

APM members get access to online publications and a 10 per cent discount on printed copies. The following publications are an example of the wide variety of topics covered:

- *APM Body of Knowledge 6th edition*
- *Governance of Co-owned Projects*
- *Directing Change*
- *Directing Agile Change*
- *APM Introduction to Programme Management 2nd edition*
- *Sponsoring Change*

These publications, and many more, can be found at apm.org.uk/book-shop

Presentations

The following presentations provide further information on managing change which may be of interest:

The common themes for successfully managing change – https://www.apm.org.uk/news/common-factors-managing-successful-change-6th-sep-2016

Understanding why people behave the way they do – https://www.apm.org.uk/news/understanding-why-people-behave-they-do-improve-change-delivery-9th-june-2016-research-report

Building internal change capability – https://www.apm.org.uk/news/degrees-of-change-the-open-university-webinar-3rd-feb-2016/

Process improvement and change management – https://www.apm.org.uk/news/process-improvement-and-change-management-29th-october-2015

Delivering effective business change – https://www.slideshare.net/assocpm/simon-williams-delivering-effective-business-change-apm-planning-for-change-240216

Changing how we change – https://www.slideshare.net/assocpm/changing-how-we-change-35570482

10

References

Adair, J. (1988) *The John Adair Handbook of Management and Leadership*, ed. N. Thomas, Thorogood, London.

APM (2014) *Conditions for Project Success*, APM, Princes Risborough.

APM (2016) Enabling Change SIG Change Pulse survey. https://www.apm.org.uk/community/enabling-change-sig/

Beer, M. and Nohria, N. (2000) 'Cracking the Code of Change', *Harvard Business Review*, 78 (3), pp.133–141, May/June 2000.

Blanchard, K.H. and Hersey, P. (1988) 'Situational Leadership: A Summary', University Associates, San Diego, CA.

Bridges, W. (1991) *Managing Transitions: Making the Most of Change*, Addison-Wesley Publishing, Reading, MA.

Cap Gemini (2016) *Accelerated Solution Environment (ASE)*, https://www.uk.capgemini.com/resources/accelerated-solutions-environment-ase

Changefirst (2016) https://www.changefirst.com/#homeslide2

Collins, J. and Porras, J. (1994) *Built to Last: Successful Habits of Visionary Companies*, HarperCollins, New York.

Conner, D. (1992) *Managing at the Speed of Change: How Resilient Managers Succeed and Prosper Where Others Fail*, Random House, New York.

Conner, D. (2012) 'The Real Story of the Burning Platform', http://www.connerpartners.com/frameworks-and-processes/the-real-story-of-the-burning-platform (Accessed 24th October 2016).

Davey, K.M. (2012) 'Evaluating Organizational Change: How and Why?' www.bbk.ac.uk/orgpsych/staff/academics/mackenzie_davey/docs/01.ppt (Accessed 30th November 2016).

Economist (2011) *Leaders of Change – Companies Prepare for a Stronger Future*, Economist Intelligence Unit, London.

Franklin, M. (2015) *Change Management Office – Benefits and Structure*, http://agilechangemanagement.co.uk/wp-content/uploads/2015/03/CMO-whitepaper-FINAL.pdf, Agile Change Management Ltd (Accessed 5th May 2017).

Goodman, E. (2013) *The Effective Team's Change Management Workbook*, RiverRhee Publishing, Royston.

Hughes, M. (2011) 'Do 70% of organisational change initiatives really fail?' http://www.bcs.org/upload/pdf/markhughes-060910.pdf (Accessed 15th January 2016).

IBM (2008) *Making Change Work*, IBM, New York.

Kotter, J.P. (1995) 'Leading Change: Why Transformation Efforts Fail', *Harvard Business Review*, 73 (2), May/June 1995.

Kotter, J.P. (1996) *Leading Change*, Harvard Business Review Press, Boston, MA.

Kotter, J.P. (2008) *A Sense of Urgency*, Harvard Business School Press, Boston, MA.

Kotter, J.P. and Cohen, D.S. (2002) *The Heart of Change*, Harvard Business Review Press, Boston, MA.

Lewin, K. (1947) 'Frontiers in group dynamics: concept, method and reality in social science, social equilibria and social change', *Human Relations*, 1 (5), June 1947.

Loveland, C.O. (2012), cited in Smith, R., 'A change management perspective', in Smith, R., King, D., Sidhu, R. and Skelsey, D. (eds) (2014) *The Effective Change Manager's Handbook*, Kogan Page, London.

McKinsey (2000) 'What successful transformations share: McKinsey Global Survey results' http://www.mckinsey.com/business-functions/organization/our-insights/what-successful-transformations-share-mckinsey-global-survey-results (Accessed 5th May 2017).

McKinsey (2008) 'Creating organisational transformations', *McKinsey Quarterly*, London.

MSP (2011) *Managing Successful Programmes*, 4th Edition, Axelos, Stationery Office.

Project Management Institute (2013), *Managing Change In Organisations: A Practice Guide*, PMI, Newton Square, PA.

Prosci (2016) *Best Practices in Change Management* , 9th Edition, Prosci, Fort Collins, CO.

Senge, P. (1990) *The Fifth Discipline: The Art and Practice of the Learning Organisation*, Doubleday, New York.

Shapiro, A. (2003) *Creating Contagious Commitment: Applying the Tipping Point to Organizational Change*, Strategy Perspective, Hillsborough, NC.

Sheen, R. and Gallo, A. (2015) *HBR Guide to Building your Business Case*, Harvard Business Review Press, Boston, MA.

Towers Watson (2013) *Change and Communication ROI Study – The 10th Anniversary Report: How the fundamentals have evolved and the best adapt*, Towers Watson, London.